Scripture in First Person, ALIVE and Off the Page

Scripture in First Person, ALIVE and Off the Page

By Lorie Forrest

2015

Dedication

This book is dedicated to Him, the Lord Jesus Christ. It's about Him and for Him; and to you, the reader, for whom the Lord moved me to write it. This book is because of Him, and it is His.

*****

Acknowledgements

I would like to thank my husband, Dean, who believed I could write a book before even I did. And to my daughter Nikki, who edited it and made these words make sense. And to my daughter Sara and my son Jason, who always believe in me, and are not surprised that I could do this!

*****

Contents

Introduction

When I first started reading the Bible years ago, I had distant feeling about God as He related to me in my life. The words of the Bible were not *to me*- they were about other people.

For a long time, He was for others and not for me. My Bible reading was sporadic and sometimes I didn't want to read it at all.

One day my husband saw that I was not taking the Bible seriously and he recommended that I change the words to be in first person.

Well I was reluctant to change God's words and dragged my feet at first, not wanting to offend God by presuming to alter His Bible; but when we changed the passage in Colossians 1:9-13 to first person, and we read it over and over, a light went on in my head!

I was able to relate to God in a way I never had before! He was actually listening to me! I was actually talking to him!

I started changing each "we'" and "His" to "I'" and "Your." I found that it didn't take anything away from the Bible; this practice actually added to it by making it personal, between Him and me.

I realized that there are many translations of the Bible out there, but nothing like this.

I hope that the words in these verses change how you can relate to God as well. If this way of reading helps just one person, I have done what God wants me to do.

I hope to show you that you, too, can take His words and read them back to Him on your own, so you can have a closer relationship with Him as I do now.

It's the change of perspective that makes the difference.

For each Scripture verse in this book, I changed the perspective to first person, followed by the original verse from the NKJ version. I organized the verses under quick reference headings for you to use when you need a more focused verse.

These are just a sampling. If your favorite verses are not included here, please try them in first person.

I also added a few hymns that are close to my heart; but not wanting to make this into a song book, I restrained myself to only these… for now!

From the beach in Progreso, Mexico,

Lorie Forrest

Author's note

The phrases in this book that are in (parentheses) are my own words from my heart. They are not my interpretations of the verse.

I would like to draw your attention to the lines you will notice between the verses.

I included these lines to suggest to you that you may want to take notes, write in your journal, or in any other way interact with your readings and reflections as you go through this book.

At some point you will begin to feel like you are talking directly to God, and that He is talking directly to you.

This will generate ideas, thoughts, and insights that you are likely to want to revisit.

Some of these verses may cause you to challenge some of your current ideas and beliefs about yourself, your God, and your relationship to Him.

I urge you to take notes in some way.

…and maybe have your Bible open next to you while you are reading this book.

Download free devotional notes and reflections sheet at

http://www.ScriptureInFirstPerson.com/devnote

Here's Where This All Started For Me

This is the first verse that I changed the reference point to first person, and it just "popped."

Now when I pray these words in first person, I feel like I'm praying to Him about issues that really affect my life right now, and I continue to read these prayers and verses because they empower me and give me confidence.

My hope is that you, when you read your Bible, would turn your favorite verses into first person and see how doing this makes them come "ALIVE and Off The Page" and into your heart!

Colossians 1:9-13

Dear Lord, fill me with the knowledge of Your will in all wisdom and spiritual understanding. Help me to walk worthy of You, Lord, fully pleasing to You, and make me fruitful in every good work, continually increasing in the knowledge of You, Lord.

Strengthen me with all might according to Your glorious power, for all patience and long-suffering with joy. I give thanks to You, Lord, who has qualified me to be a partaker of the inheritance of Your saints in the light.

Thank You, Lord, for delivering me from the power of darkness and conveying me into the kingdom of the Son of Your love. Amen!

_____

_____

_____

_____

_____

Colossians 1:9-13

For this reason we also, since the day we heard it, do not cease to pray for you, and to ask that you may be filled with the knowledge of His will in all wisdom and spiritual understanding;

that you may walk worthy of the Lord, fully pleasing Him, being fruitful in every good work and increasing in the knowledge of God; strengthened with all might, according to His glorious power, for all patience and long-suffering with joy;

giving thanks to the Father who has qualified us to be partakers of the inheritance of the saints in the light.

He has delivered us from the power of darkness and conveyed us into the kingdom of the Son of His love.

Because I Am Special to You, God

**Zephaniah 3:17 | 2 Chronicles 16:9a
Deuteronomy 7:6-9 | Psalm 8:3-5 | Psalm 34:4-9
Isaiah 43:1-4 | Romans 8:37-39 | Hebrews 13:20-
21   Ephesians 1:2-10 | Ephesians 2:1-8 | Psalm
100   1 John 5:1-3**

*****

These verses and passages help me to see just how much He really does love me! These words are so beautiful to me. They are great helps when I need to feel included in His world and when I need to know that He really is with me all the time.

He rejoices over you and me with singing! How awesome is that?

Zephaniah 3:17

You, Lord, are near me. You are the Mighty One who saves. You will rejoice over me with gladness! You quiet me with Your love and You rejoice over me with singing.

(Thank You, Lord, for Your promises! Thank You for Your Presence in my life! Amen.)

_____

_____

_____

_____

_____

Zephaniah 3:17

The Lord your God is in your midst, the Mighty one, will save; He will rejoice over you with gladness, He will quiet you with His love, He will rejoice over you with singing.

When I first read this next verse the way it was originally written, I went right by it, not even noticing it. I did not believe it could be about me! How could He be searching and seeking for me?

It wasn't until I accepted that He really does love me in this way that I saw it.

Then I realized, "Why not me?" …And why not you?

2 Chronicles 16:9a

Your eyes, Lord, run to and fro throughout the whole earth, to show Yourself strong for me, because my heart is loyal to You.

_____

_____

_____

_____

_____

2 Chronicles 16:9

For the eyes of the Lord run to and fro throughout the whole earth, to show Himself strong on behalf of those whose heart is loyal to Him.

This passage really hits my heart, because in it He tells me (the way I read it) that I am a special treasure to Him. It means so much to me that He says that about me, His creation!

How do you feel being God's special treasure?

Deuteronomy 7:6-9

I am holy to You, my King! You have chosen me to be Yours; I am a special treasure to You. You have set Your love on me!

I know that You, God, are my God, faithful and true. You keep Your promises for a thousand generations to those (including me) who love You and keep Your commandments.

(I thank You, Lord, for loving me before I was even born!)

_____

_____

_____

_____

_____

Deuteronomy 7:6-9

For you are a holy people to the Lord your God; the Lord your God has chosen you to be a people for Himself, a special treasure, above all the peoples on the face of the earth.

The Lord did not set His love on you nor choose you because you were more in number than any other people, for you were the least of all peoples;

but because the Lord loves you, and because He would keep the oath which He swore to your fathers, the Lord has brought you out with a mighty hand, and redeemed you from the house of bondage, from the hand of Pharaoh king of Egypt.

Therefore, know that the Lord your God, He is God, the faithful God who keeps covenant and mercy for a thousand generations with those who love him and keep his commandments.

In this passage, I see that you and I are special treasures to Him. He was mindful of us even while He was busy working to create all the beautiful things we see all around.

We're just as special as everything else He made - He has crowned us with glory and honor!

Psalm 8:3-5

When I consider Your heavens, the work of Your fingers, the moon and the stars, which You have ordained, I thank You that You are mindful of me, and I thank You that You visit me.

Thank You that You have made me a little lower than the angels and that You have crowned me with glory and honor. Amen!

_____
_____
_____
_____

Psalm 8:3-5

When I consider Your heavens, the work of Your fingers, the moon and the stars, which You have ordained, What is man that you are mindful of him, and the son of man that you visit him?

For You have made him a little lower than the angels and You have crowned him with glory and honor.

Psalm 34:4-9

When I seek You, You hear me and deliver me from all my fears. When I look to You, I am radiant to You and You see no shame in me.

Oh, Lord, when I cry out to You, You hear me and save me from all of my troubles! You are with me. You guard me and deliver me, because I fear You, (my King)!

Oh, I have tasted and seen that You, Lord, are good, and I am blessed because I trust in You! There is nothing I need besides You and what You want me to have.

_____

_____

_____

_____

_____

Psalm 34:4-9

I sought the Lord, and He heard me, and delivered me from all my fears. They looked to Him and were radiant, and their faces were not ashamed. This poor man cried out, and the Lord heard him, and saved him out of all his troubles.

The angel of the Lord encamps all around those who fear Him, and delivers them. Oh, taste and see that the Lord is good; blessed is the man who trusts in Him! O fear the Lord, you his saints! There is no want to those who fear Him.

I can have no fear at all when I read this; it is like a lifeline to me! No matter what I go through, He's right there!

What verse makes you feel safe like this one does for me?

Isaiah 43:1-4

You formed me. I will not fear because You have redeemed me, You have called me by name; I am Yours. When I pass through the waters, You will be with me, and the waters will not overtake me.

When I walk through fire, I will not be burned. You are my Lord, the Holy One, my Savior. I am precious in Your sight. I am honored and You love me. Amen!

_____

_____

_____

_____

_____

Isaiah 43:1-4

But now, thus says the Lord, that created you, O Jacob, and He who formed you, O Israel: fear not, for I have redeemed you; I have called you by your name; you are Mine.

When you pass through the waters, I will be with you; and through the rivers, they shall not overflow you. When you walk through the fire, you shall not be burned, nor shall the flame scorch you.

For I am the Lord your God, the Holy One of Israel, your Savior; I gave Egypt for your ransom, Ethiopia and Seba in your place. Since you are precious in My sight, you have been honored, and I have loved you; therefore I will give men for you, and people for your life.

Romans 8:37-39

In difficult times, I am a conqueror through You. Because You love me, I am more than a conqueror.

I am persuaded that neither death nor life, nor angels, nor principalities, nor powers, nor things present, nor things to come, nor height, nor depth, nor any other created thing, shall be able to separate me from the love You have for me in Jesus!

_____

_____

_____

_____

_____

Romans 8:37-39

Yet in all these things we are more than conquerors through Him who loved us. For I am persuaded that neither death nor life, nor angels nor principalities nor powers, nor things present nor things to come, nor height nor depth, nor any other created thing, shall be able to separate us from the love of God which is in Christ Jesus our Lord.

Hebrews 13:20-21

Dear Lord, my God of Peace, who brought my King up from the dead, my great Shepherd, through the blood of the everlasting covenant, make me complete in every good work.

Help me finish the work You want me to do, follow Your will, and be pleasing in Your sight. To You, Jesus Christ, be the glory forever and ever. Amen.

_____

_____

_____

_____

_____

Hebrews 13:20-21

Now may the God of peace who brought up our Lord Jesus from the dead, that great Shepherd of the sheep, through the blood of the everlasting covenant,

make you complete in every good work to do His will, working in you what is well pleasing in His sight, through Jesus Christ, to whom be glory forever and ever, amen.

Ephesians 1:2-10

Thank You for Your grace and peace. You have blessed me with every spiritual blessing that is with You in the heavenly places. You chose me to remain in You before the foundation of the world, that I should be holy and blameless before You in love.

I believe that You predestined me and adopted me into Your family as Your child, according to the good pleasure of Your will. I praise You, God, that because of Your grace, You made me acceptable to You, my Beloved.

Thank You for giving me redemption through Your blood, the forgiveness of my sins, and the richness of Your grace, which You made to abound toward me in all wisdom and understanding.

I pray that You bring unity to all things in heaven and on earth under Your power.

_____

_____

_____

_____

_____

Ephesians 1:2-10

Grace to you and peace from God our father and the Lord Jesus Christ. Blessed be the God and Father of our Lord Jesus Christ, who has blessed us with every spiritual blessing in the heavenly places in Christ,

just as He chose us in Him before the foundation of the world, that we should be holy and without blame before Him in love, having predestined us to adoption as sons by Jesus Christ to Himself, according to the good pleasure of His will, to the praise of the glory of His grace, by which he made us accepted in the beloved.

In Him we have redemption through His blood, the forgiveness of sins, according to the riches of His grace which He made to abound toward us and all wisdom and prudence having made known to us the mystery of His will,

according to his good pleasure which He proposed in Himself, that in the dispensation of the fullness of the times He might gather together in one all things in Christ, both which are in heaven and which are on earth-in Him.

We could never have done anything to make Him save us. He saved us just because He wanted to! His grace is a gift you and I have and gladly accept!

Ephesians 2:1-8

Thank You for making me alive when I was once dead! Thank You for taking from me my trespasses and sins, in which I used to walk.

Because You love me, God, and because You are so rich in mercy and love even though I was dead in sin, You made me alive, together with You, my Lord Jesus.

I have been raised up and made to sit in heavenly places! Thank You, Lord, for giving me full confidence – not for anything that I have done, but just because You wanted to.

For by grace I have been saved, through faith – and it is not from me; it is a gift from You, Lord! (Thank You, Lord!)

_____

_____

_____

_____

_____

Ephesians 2:1-8

And you He made alive, who were dead in trespasses and sins, in which you once walked according to the course of this world according to the prince of the power of the air, the spirit who now works in the sons of disobedience,

among whom also we all once conducted ourselves in the lusts of our flesh, fulfilling the desires of the flesh and of the mind and were by nature children of wrath, just as the others.

But God who is rich in mercy because of His great love with which He loved us, even when we were dead in trespasses, made us alive together with Christ (by grace you have been saved)and raised us up together, and made us sit together in the heavenly places in Christ Jesus,

that in the ages to come He might show the acceding riches of His grace in His kindness toward us in Christ Jesus for by grace you have been saved through faith, and that not of yourselves; it is the gift of God.

Psalm 100

You make my heart happy! I worship You with gladness, and I come before You singing with joy! You are my God; You made me, and I am Yours (and You are mine). I am a sheep in your pasture.

I always enter Your gates with thanksgiving and go into Your courts with praise! I thank You and bless Your name, because You, Lord, are good!

(Your love is unfailing), and Your mercy is everlasting. Your truth continues to each generation, (even mine)! Amen.

_____

_____

_____

_____

_____

Psalm 100

Make a joyful shout to the Lord, all you lands! Serve the Lord with gladness; come before His presence with singing.

Know that the Lord, He is God; it is He who has made us, and not we ourselves; we are His people and the sheep of His pasture. Enter into His gates with thanksgiving and to His courts with praise.

Be thankful to Him, and bless His name. For the Lord is good; His mercy is everlasting, and His truth endures to all generations.

Sometimes it is so hard to obey Him (sometimes my thoughts really distract me), but when I realize that He is keeping me safe from myself, it's much easier to obey His Word!

1 John 5:1-3

I believe that You, Jesus, are the Christ, born of God. When I love You, I also love Your Father who made me.

By this I know that I am Your child: I love You, God, and I keep Your commandments; Your commandments are not burdensome to me. (Thank You for saving me, Lord!) Amen!

_____

_____

_____

_____

_____

1 John 5:1-3

Whoever believes that Jesus is the Christ is born of God, and everyone who loves Him who begot, also loves him who is begotten of him. By this I know that we love the children of God, when we love God and keep His commandments. For this is the love of God, that we keep his commandments. And his commandments are not burdensome.

My God Gives Me Wisdom

**Colossians 2:2-3 | Psalm 15 | Ephesians 1:17-23
Colossians 3:12-17 | Luke 24:32, 45 | James 1:19-
22**

*****

There are so many verses in the Bible about getting and seeking wisdom. Our Father thought of everything when He gave us His Word, and He knows us so well! Here are just some of the verses and passages that help me so much. They are His gifts to me and my gifts to you!

Colossians 2:2-3

Father in heaven, I pray with all my heart that I would be encouraged and knit together with my brothers and sisters in Jesus, in Your love, so that I will have the full riches of the assurance of understanding of Your Word.

I want to know the mystery of You, God, both You and my Lord Jesus, because in You are all the hidden treasures of wisdom and knowledge. Thank You! In Jesus' name, amen.

_____

_____

_____

_____

_____

Colossians 2:2-3

That their hearts may be encouraged, being knit together in love, and attaining to all riches of the full assurance of understanding, to the knowledge of the mystery of God, both of the Father and of Christ, in whom are hidden all the treasures of wisdom and knowledge.

Psalm 15

Dear Lord, I dwell in Your tabernacle and on Your holy hill. I pray that I will walk uprightly and I am righteous in Your sight. Help me speak only the truth from my heart, O Lord.

Keep me from being a backbiter and stay my tongue. Keep me from doing evil to my neighbor and from judging my friends.

Help me avoid people who despise You, and stay close to those who honor and fear You, Lord. Help me keep my promises, no matter what.

I give generously whenever I have the means to help. I help those whom I can help.

(In Your precious name I pray), amen.

_____

_____

_____

_____

Psalm 15

A Psalm of David

Lord, who may abide in Your tabernacle? Who may dwell in Your holy hill? He who walks uprightly, and works righteousness, and speaks the truth in his heart;

He who does not back bite with his tongue, nor does evil to his neighbor, nor does he take up a reproach against his friend; In whose eyes a vile person is despised, but he honors those who fear the Lord;

he who swears to his own hurt and does not change; he who does not put out his money at usury, nor does he take a bribe against the innocent. He who does these things shall never be moved.

Ephesians 1:17-23

Dear Lord, give me the spirit of wisdom and revelation. Give me understanding that I might comprehend Your Word so that I can know You better.

Enlighten the eyes of my heart in order that I may know the hope of Your calling, the glory of my inheritance, and the greatness of Your power towards me.

I believe in Your great power, the same power that raised You, my Lord, from the dead.

And now You are seated at our Father's right hand in the heavenly realms, far above all rule and authority, power and dominion.

Father, You placed everything under Jesus' feet and You appointed Him to be head over everything for the church, which is His body.

The fullness of Him fills everything in every way. Praise to You, Lord. Amen.

_____

_____

_____

_____

_____

Ephesians 1:17-23

That the God of our Lord Jesus Christ, the Father of glory, may give you the spirit of wisdom and revelation in the knowledge of Him, the eyes of your understanding being enlightened;

that you may know what is the hope of His calling, what are the riches of the glory of his inheritance in the saints, and what is the exceeding greatness of His power toward us who believe,

according to the working of His mighty power which He worked in Christ when He raised Him from the dead and seated Him at his right hand in the heavenly places, far above all principality and power and might and dominion and every name that is named, not only in this age but also and that is to come.

And He put all things under His feet, and gave Him to be head over all things to the church which is His body, the fullness of Him who fills all in all.

Colossians 3:12-17

Dear Lord, I thank You that, because You elected me (before the world was even created), I am holy and loved! Help me demonstrate tender mercies, kindness, humility, meekness, and patience, bearing with others and forgiving others just as You forgive me.

But above all things, I put on love, which binds all these things together in perfect unity. Peace, Your peace, rules in my heart. Thank You, God, for putting Your Word in me richly, with all wisdom, and for teaching and admonishing me.

I sing to You with psalms and hymns and spiritual songs and with grace in my heart. Whatever I do, in word or deed, I do all in Your name my Lord Jesus, always giving thanks to You, God my Father! In Your name I pray, amen.

_____

_____

_____

_____

_____

Colossians 3:12-17

Therefore, as the elect of God, holy and beloved, put on tender mercies, kindness, humility, meekness, and long-suffering; bearing with one another, and forgiving one another, if anyone

has a complaint against another; even as Christ forgave you, so you also must do.

But above all these things put on love, which is the bond of perfection. And let the peace of God rule in your hearts, to which also you were called in one body; and be thankful. Let the word of Christ dwell in you richly in all wisdom, teaching and admonishing one another in psalms and hymns and spiritual songs, singing with grace in your hearts to the Lord.

And whatever you do in word or deed, do all in the name of the Lord Jesus, giving thanks to God the Father through Him.

I combined two verses here. Together, they help me pray these words even more clearly. I think the verses complement each other very well.

Luke 24:32, 45

Dear Lord, my heart burns within me when I hear Your voice. (As I open Your Word every day), open my understanding that I might comprehend Your Scriptures!

(Let me hear You clearly! Your words are so beautiful to me!)

Thank You, Lord.

_____

_____

_____

_____

_____

Luke 24:32,45

And they said to one another, did not our heart burn within us while He talked with us on the road, and while He opened the Scriptures to us?

...and He opened their understanding, that they might comprehend the Scriptures.

James 1:19-22

Dear Lord, make me quick to hear, slow to speak, and slow to anger, because my anger does not produce Your righteousness, God.

Therefore, I lay aside all filthiness and wickedness and receive with meekness Your implanted Word, which is able to save my soul.

Help me be a doer of Your Word and not just a hearer only, deceiving myself.

In Jesus' name, Amen.

_____

_____

_____

_____

_____

James 1:19-22

My beloved brethren, let every man be swift to hear, slow to speak, slow to wrath; for the wrath of man does not produce the righteousness of God.

Therefore, lay aside all filthiness and overflow of wickedness, and receive with meekness the implanted word, which is able to save your souls.

But be doers of the word and not hearers only, deceiving yourselves.

Walking With My God

**Joshua 22:5 | 1 Chronicles 28:9 | Mark 11:22-24
Luke 9:56 | Luke 11:9-10 | John 10:27-28
Romans 5:1-2 | John 15:1-8 | John 15:7-13
Romans 10:8-9 | 1 Corinthians 15:58
Ephesians 3:14-19 | Ephesians 3:20-21
Ephesians 4:1-3 | Hebrews 4:12-13 | James 1:17-
18   2 Peter 1:1-4 | Ephesians 5:8-10**

*****

Walking with Him is so much easier than walking without Him, isn't it? Because of His grace and forgiveness, we can always walk right next to Him!

Joshua 22:5

I am careful to heed what Your commandments tell me. I love You, my Lord and my God,

I am careful to walk in all your ways, to keep Your commandments, and hold fast to You, my Savior.

Help me serve You with all my heart and all my soul.

Joshua 22:5

But take careful heed to do the commandment and the law which Moses the servant of the Lord commanded you, to love the Lord your God,

to walk in all His ways, to keep His commandments, to hold fast to Him, and to serve Him with all your heart and with all your soul.

1 Chronicles 28:9

Since I am Your child, I will know You, Father, more every day. I will serve You with a loyal heart and with a willing mind.

Lord, search my heart and know my thoughts and my intentions. When I seek You, I will find You. I pray that I will never forsake You and that You keep me forever. Amen.

_____

_____

_____

_____

_____

1 Chronicles 28:9

As for you, My son Solomon, know the God of your father, and serve Him with a loyal heart and with a willing mind; for the Lord searches all hearts and understands all the intent of the thoughts. If you seek Him, He will be found by you; but if you forsake Him, He will cast you off forever.

Mark 11:22-24

Dear Lord, (please give me a strong faith). Because of the faith I have in You, if I tell a mountain to be removed and cast into the sea, and do not doubt in my heart, but believe that You will do it, it will be done for me.

Thank You that whatever I ask for and believe that You have given to me already, I have it!

_____

_____

_____

_____

_____

Mark 11:22-24

So Jesus answered and said to them, have faith in God. For surely, I say to you, whoever says to this mountain, be removed and be cast into the sea, and does not doubt in his heart, but believes that those things he says will be done, he will have whatever he says. Therefore, I say to you, whatever things you ask when you pray, believe that you receive them, and you will have them.

Luke 9:56

Dear Lord, You did not come to destroy my life, but to save it. (Lord, make me a blessing for You wherever I go. Amen!)

_____

_____

_____

_____

_____

Luke 9:56

For the Son of Man did not come to destroy men's lives but to save them, and they went to another village.

Luke 11:9-10

Dear Lord, You have told me that when I ask, I will receive; when I seek, I will find; when I knock, it will be opened to me.

So I know when I ask, I receive; when I seek, I find; and when I knock, it will be opened!

(I thank You for repeating this to make sure that I understand and believe You.)

_____

_____

_____

_____

_____

Luke 11:9-10

So I say to you, ask, and it will be given to you; seek and you will find; knock, and it will be opened to you.

Everyone who asks receives and he who seeks finds, and to him who knocks it will be opened.

John 10:27-28

Dear Lord, I hear Your voice, and You know me, and I will follow You. You gave me eternal life; I will never die, nor shall anyone snatch me out of Your hand.

(I am Yours! Thank You for Your promises!)

_____

_____

_____

_____

_____

John 10: 27-28

My sheep hear my voice, and I know them, and they follow me. And I will give them eternal life, and they shall never perish; neither shall anyone snatch them out of my hand.

Romans 5:1-2

Dear Lord, because I have been justified by faith, I have peace with You, my Lord Jesus Christ, through whom I also have access by faith into our Father's grace in which I stand.

I rejoice in the hope of the glory that You promise to me. Thank You, Lord, for saving me!

_____

_____

_____

_____

_____

Romans 5:1-2

Therefore, having been justified by faith, we have peace with God through our Lord Jesus Christ, through whom also we have access by faith into this grace in which we stand, and rejoice in hope of the glory of God.

When I abide in Him, He abides in me. I know how true His Word is. Whenever I go a few days without reading His Word, I feel disconnected and apart from Him.

How about you? Have you ever noticed this in your own walk with Him?

John 15:1-8

Dear Lord Jesus, You are the true vine, and our Father is the vine dresser. Every branch in You that does not bear fruit, our Father takes away.

Prune every branch in me that does not bear fruit so that I might bear even more fruit.

I am clean because Your words are in me. When I abide in You, You abide in me. I cannot bear fruit unless I abide in You and You in me. You are the vine; I am the branches.

When I abide in You and You in me, I am able to bear much fruit in You; apart from You I can do nothing.

When I am not in You, I wither. So I abide in You and Your words abide in me. Thank You that whatever I desire in You will be done.

By this our Father is glorified: that I bear much fruit, so I am Your disciple.

_____

_____

_____

_____

John 15:1-8

I am the true vine, and My Father is the vine dresser. Every branch in Me that does not bear fruit He takes away; and every branch that bears fruit He prunes, that it may bear more fruit. You are already clean because of the word which I have spoken to you.

Abide in Me, and I in you. As the branch cannot bear fruit of itself, unless it's abides in the vine, neither can you, unless you abide in Me. I am the vine, you are the branches. He who abides in Me, and I in Him, bears much fruit; for without Me you can do nothing.\

If anyone does not abide in Me, he is cast out as a branch and is withered; and they gather them and throw them into the fire and they are burned. If you abide in Me, and My words abide in you, you will ask for what you desire, and it shall be done for you.

By this my Father is glorified, that you bear much fruit; so you will be My disciples.

John 15:7-13

Dear Lord Jesus, when I abide in You and Your words abide in me, whatever I ask for is done for me. By this our Father is glorified: that I am bearing much fruit through my life, and I am Your disciple.

As our Father loves You, Jesus, You love me, and I abide in Your love. I keep Your commandments, abiding in Your love, just as You keep our Father's commands and abide in His love. You teach me these things, so that Your joy will remain in me, and that my joy will be full.

Your commandment to me is to love others as You have loved me. You showed me that there's no greater love than when You laid down Your life for me!

(Help me love others in my heart and show them Your love through me.) Amen.

_____

_____

_____

_____

_____

John 15:7-13

If you abide in Me, and My words abide in you, you will ask what you desire, and it shall be done for you. By this My Father is glorified, that you bear much fruit; so you will be My disciples.

As the Father loved Me, I also have loved you; abide in My love. If you keep My commandments, you will abide in My love, just as I have kept My Father's Commandments and abide in His love.

These things I have spoken to you, that My joy may remain in you, and that your joy may be full. This is my commandment, that you love one another as I have loved you. Greater love has no one than this then to lay down one's life for his friends.

Romans 10:8-9

Dear Lord, Your Word is near me, in my mouth and in my heart. Since I confess with my mouth that You are the Lord, and believe in my heart that God has raised You from the dead, I am saved! (I believe!)

Thank You, Lord, for saving me! In Jesus' name, Amen!

_____

_____

_____

_____

_____

Romans 10:8-9

But what does it say? "The word is near you, in your mouth and in your heart" (that is, the word of faith which we preach) that if you confess with your mouth the Lord Jesus and believe in your heart that God has raised Him from the dead, you will be saved.

This was my theme verse while writing this book. I leaned on it to get me through the slow times when I felt like giving up. He is faithful, faithful to the end!

1 Corinthians 15:58

Dear Lord, make me steadfast and immovable, always abounding in the work You have for me. I know that my labor is not in vain when I am working on the tasks You have for me.

(I pray for Your patience when I feel like I am doing Your work more slowly than I think I should be. In Your Name I pray, amen.)

_____

_____

_____

_____

_____

1 Corinthians 15:58

Therefore, my beloved brethren, be steadfast, immovable, always abounding in the work of the Lord, knowing that your labor is not in vain in the Lord.

This is such a beautiful passage that shows just how much He cares for us! He continues to show me every day when He puts all of His power and love on me, and how complete I am when I am empowered by Him!

Do you see this care in your own life?

Ephesians 3:14-19

Dear Lord, when I think of all the things You do for me, I fall to my knees and pray to You, Father, the Creator of everything in heaven and earth.

From Your glorious, unlimited resources, empower me with inner strength through Your Spirit. My Lord Jesus, make Your home in my heart as I trust in You in my true self

Make my roots grow deep, being grounded in Your love so that I am able to understand how wide, how long, how high and how deep Your love for me is.

And let me know and deeply experience Your love, my Lord Jesus, so that I am filled with all the fullness God! In Your Name I pray, amen.

_____

_____

_____

_____

_____

Ephesians 3:14-19

For this reason I bow my knees to the Father of our Lord Jesus Christ, from whom the whole family in heaven and earth is named, that He would grant you, according to the riches of His glory, to be strengthened with might through His Spirit in the inner man,

that Christ may dwell in your hearts through faith; that you, being rooted and grounded in love, may be able to comprehend with all the saints what is the width and length and depth and height,

to know the love of Christ which passes knowledge; that you may be filled with all the fullness of God.

Ephesians 3:20-21

To You, my God, who are able to do exceedingly abundantly above all that I ask or think according to Your power that works in me, to You be the glory in the church by Christ Jesus to all generations, forever and ever. Amen.

_____

_____

_____

_____

_____

Ephesians 3:20-21

Now to Him who is able to do exceedingly abundantly above all that we ask or think, according to the power that works in us, to him be glory in the church by Christ Jesus to all generations, forever and ever. Amen.

Ephesians 4:1-3

Dear Lord, help me walk worthy of the calling with which I was called, with all humility and gentleness, with patience, bearing with others in love, endeavoring to keep the unity of Your Spirit in the bond of peace.

(I do these things through Your strength and not my own.) In Your name, amen.

_____

_____

_____

_____

_____

Ephesians 4:1-3

I, therefore, the prisoner of the Lord, beseech you to walk worthy of the calling with which you were called, with all lowliness and gentleness, with long-suffering, bearing with one another in love, endeavoring to keep the unity of the Spirit in the bond of peace.

In this passage, I can really see the warrior in Him shine through!

Hebrews 4:12-13

Dear God, Your Word living in me is more powerful and sharper than any two-edged sword, piercing even between my soul and spirit, and joints and marrow.

Your Word is a discerner of the thoughts and intents of my heart. I cannot hide from Your sight, but in all things, I am naked and open to Your eyes, my Father, to whom I must give account.

_____

_____

_____

_____

_____

Hebrews 4:12-13

For the word of God is living and powerful, and sharper than any two- edged sword, piercing even to the division of soul and spirit, and of joints and marrow,

and is a discerner of the thoughts and intents of the heart and if there is no creature hidden from His sight, but all things are naked and open to the eyes of Him to whom we must give account.

James 1:17-18

Dear Lord, (I am grateful and thankful to You, for) every good and perfect gift is from above, and comes down to me from You, Father of lights.

With You there is no change or shadow of turning. You never change!

Of Your own free will, You brought me to You by the Word of truth, that I might be a kind of first fruits of Your creatures! (Help me bear good fruit for You, Lord.) Amen.

_____

_____

_____

_____

_____

James 1:17-18

Every good gift and every perfect gift is from above, and comes down from the Father of lights, with whom there is no variation or shadow of turning. Of His own will He brought us forth by the word of truth, that we might be a kind of first fruits of His creatures.

2 Peter 1:1-4

Lord Jesus my Savior, I am Your servant. I have obtained precious faith through Your righteousness! May grace and peace grow in me in abundance as my knowledge of You grows.

Through Your divine power, and through the knowledge of You, You have given to me everything I need for a godly life. You called me by Your own glory and goodness.

Through my growing knowledge of You and Your great and precious promises, I participate in Your divine nature, having escaped the corruption of the world caused by evil desires.

_____

_____

_____

_____

_____

2 Peter 1:1-4

Simon Peter, a bondservant and apostle of Jesus Christ, to those who have obtained like precious faith with us by the righteousness of our God and Savior Jesus Christ:

Grace and peace be multiplied to you in the knowledge of God and of Jesus our Lord, as his divine power has given to us all things that pertain to life and godliness, through the knowledge of him who called us by glory and virtue,

by which have been given to us exceedingly great and precious promises, that through these you may be partakers of the divine nature, having escaped the corruption that is in the world through lust.

Ephesians 5:8-10

For I was once darkness, but now I am light in the Lord.

Now I live as a child of that light, and bear the Spiritual fruit that light brings. I have Your goodness, righteousness, and truth in me, and I keep finding out what pleases You!

_____

_____

_____

_____

Ephesians 5:8-10

For you were once darkness, but now you are light in the Lord. Walk as children of light (for the fruit of the spirit is in all goodness, righteousness, and truth), finding out what is acceptable to the Lord.

My God is Always With Me

Exodus 15:2-3 | Isaiah 46:4 | Galatians 2:20
Psalm 119:114 | 2 Thessalonians 3:2-5 | 1 John 3:1
Deuteronomy 6:5-6 | John 3:15-18

*****

I can do nothing apart from Him! When I read and pray these verses and passages, I feel His presence. I know that He is always there for me, and He always will be!

He is my Warrior! He is my strength! I find that I go to Him more when I look to Him in this light, as "my Warrior."

Do you have a favorite way to think of Him?

Exodus 15:2-3

Dear Lord, You are my strength and my defense. (Help me when I am in trouble.) You are my salvation and song!

You are my God, and I praise you, my Father and my God! I exalt You! You are my warrior!

_____

_____

_____

_____

_____

Exodus 15:2-3

The Lord is my strength and song, and He has become my salvation; He is my God, and I will praise Him; my Father's God, and I will exalt Him. The Lord is a man of war; the Lord is His name.

Isaiah 46:4

Dear Lord, You will be my God throughout my lifetime, until my hair is white with age. You made me and You will care for me!

Thank You for being the One to carry me along this life and to save me!

(You are the Mighty One who controls everything!)

_____

_____

_____

_____

_____

Isaiah 46:4

Even to your old age, I am He, and even to gray hairs I will carry you! I have made, and will bear; even I will carry, and will deliver you.

I remember when I was first going to church, there was a very godly man who, at every opportunity, would stand up and recite this verse, word for word.

And the look on his face was so beautiful! It brought me to tears when I saw how much he loved God! And how much God loved him!

I have the pleasure of knowing now that this verse is for me, too! Amazing love, how can it be!

Galatians 2:20

(Dear Lord, I am grateful for what You have done for me. You have died for me, and I died with You in that same moment! So then, I can say with confidence:)

I have been crucified with You, Lord Jesus. It is no longer I who live, but it is You who live in me; and the life which I now live in the flesh, I live by faith in You, Jesus.

You loved me and You gave Yourself for me! Thank You, my Savior!

_____

_____

_____

_____

_____

Galatians 2:20

I have been crucified with Christ; it is no longer I who live, but Christ lives in me; and the life which I now live in the flesh I live by faith in the Son of God, who loved me and gave Himself for me.

Here's one that is already in first person, but I felt that the words were so beautiful, I just couldn't resist including it!

Psalm 119:114

Dear Lord, You are my hiding place and my shield; I hope in Your Word.

(I always put my hope in You. Hold me up and I shall be safe. I trust in You! Because I seek You, You will be in my life! I pray this in Your name, amen.)

_____

_____

_____

_____

_____

Psalm 119:114

You are my hiding place and my shield; I hope in your word.

2 Thessalonians 3:2-5

Dear Lord, deliver me from wicked and evil people; not everyone has faith in Your name. Lord, You are faithful! You strengthen me and protect me from the evil one.

I have confidence in You, Lord, concerning me, that I do and will do the things You want me to do.

Direct my heart towards Your love and the patience that is in You! Thank You, Holy One! Amen.

_____

_____

_____

_____

_____

2 Thessalonians 3:2-5

And that we may be delivered from unreasonable and wicked men; for not all have faith. But the Lord is faithful, who will establish you and guard you from the evil one.

And we have confidence in the Lord concerning you, both that you do and will do the things we command you.

Now may the Lord direct your hearts into the love of God and into the patience of Christ.

Having never had a father, I could never relate to this verse until I truly accepted Him for who He is: my Father. And I am His child! It never ceases to amaze me that He is my Father just because He wants to be!

1 John 3:1

Dear Lord, I am in awe when I behold the manner of love You have bestowed on me, that I can be called Your child.

(Lord, help me live as Your child should live. I am always grateful to You for wanting to be my Father. I could do nothing on my own to deserve it. You bestowed on me the right to be called a child of God to save me!)

Thank You for Your precious promises! Amen!

_____

_____

_____

_____

_____

1 John 3:1

Behold what manner of love the Father has bestowed on us, that we should be called children of God! Therefore, the world does not know us, because it did not know Him.

Deuteronomy 6:5-6

Dear Lord, I love You, my God, with all my heart, with all my soul, and with all my strength.

Keep these words in my heart always. In Your precious name I pray, amen.

_____

_____

_____

_____

_____

Deuteronomy 6:5-6

You shall love the Lord your God with all your heart, with all your soul, and with all your strength. And these words which I command you today shall be in your heart.

This passage is so well known that almost every Christian knows it by heart. But have you ever said it like this? Like it is meant just for you? Doesn't it bring the passage closer to home?

John 3:15-18

Dear Lord, I believe in You. I believe You died for my sins. Because I believe this, I will not die but have eternal life.

For You, God, loved me so much that You gave Your only son for me so that, believing in You, I will not perish, but have everlasting life.

You did not send Your son condemn me, but to save me. Because I believe in You, I am not condemned – I am saved! Thank You, Lord, for Your promises! Amen!

_____

_____

_____

_____

_____

John 3:15-18

That whoever believes in him should not perish but have eternal life. For God so loved the world that He gave His only begotten son, that whoever believes in Him should not perish but have everlasting life.

For God did not send His Son into the world to condemn the world, but that the world through Him might be saved. He who believes in Him is not condemned; but he who does not believe is condemned already, because he has not believed in the name of the only begotten Son of God.

When I Need Confidence in You, Lord

**Psalm 91 | Numbers 6:24-26 | Proverbs 3:5-8
Jeremiah 29:11-13 | 1 John 4:7-11 | 1 John 5:14-15
Habakkuk 3:18-19 | Exodus 33:12-14**

*****

These are some of my favorite passages and verses! He wants me to have the utmost confidence in Him and to rely on Him for my every decision, and when I read these, I know that He is there with me and for me, no matter what!

I love this chapter! This is my favorite in the whole Bible! He is my secret place, and when I abide under His shadow, He is my refuge! He covers me with His love and He keeps me safe!

If by chance, you don't have a favorite Bible verse or chapter, I offer this one for your consideration.

Psalm 91

When I dwell in Your secret place, Most High, and I abide under Your shadow, You, God, are my refuge and fortress! You are my God and I trust in You. You deliver me from any traps I fall into and from any evil that comes near me.

You cover me with Your feathers, and I take refuge under Your wings. Your truth is a shield to me! I am not afraid of the dark or of anything I can see, or any evil that comes near me, day or night, because I have made You, Lord, my refuge and dwelling place.

You give Your angels charge over me to keep me in all my ways; in their hands, they bear me up so I am not tempted.

Because I have set my love on You, You deliver me and hold me up, and when I call on You, You answer me. Be with me, my Lord, when I'm troubled and deliver me with a long life.

Show me Your salvation! In Your name, I pray, Amen.

_____

_____

_____

_____

_____

Psalm 91

He who dwells in the secret place of the Most High shall abide under the shadow of the Almighty. I will say to the Lord, "He is my refuge and my fortress; My God, in Him I will trust."

Surely He shall deliver you from the snare of the fowler and from the perilous pestilence. He shall cover you with His feathers, and under His wings you shall take refuge; His truth shall be your shield and buckler.

You shall not be afraid of the terror by night, nor of the arrow that flies by the day, nor of the pestilence that walks in the darkness, nor of the destruction that lays waste at noon day. A thousand may fall at your side, and ten thousand at your right hand; But it shall not come near you.

Only with your eyes shall you look, and see the reward of the wicked. Because you have made the Lord, who is my refuge, even the Most High, your dwelling place, no evil shall befall you, nor shall any plague come near your dwelling;

For He shall give His angels charge over you, To keep you in all your ways. In their hands they shall bear you up, lest you dash your foot against a stone. You shall tread upon the lion and the cobra, the young lion and the serpent you shall trample under foot.

"Because he has set his love Me, therefore I will deliver him I will set him on high, because he has known My name. He shall call upon Me, and I will answer him;

I will be with him in trouble; I will deliver him and honor him. With long life I will satisfy him, and show him My salvation.

Numbers 6:24-26

You bless me and keep me. You make Your face shine upon me. And You are gracious to me, Lord; You smile upon me, and give me peace.

(Thank You for Your precious words and promises! In Your name I pray, amen!)

_____

_____

_____

_____

_____

Numbers 6:24-26

The Lord bless you and keep you; The Lord make his face shine upon you, and be gracious to you; The Lord lift up his countenance upon you, and give you peace.

This passage is so present and evident in my life. So often, I try to do things on my own and with my own understanding, and I mess up time and time again.

I'm so glad He is there for us to turn to.

Proverbs 3:5-8

Father in heaven, I trust in You with all my heart, and I do not lean on my own understanding; but in all my ways, I acknowledge You, and You direct my paths.

I pray that I will never be wise in my own eyes, but that I will fear You in my heart and turn from evil. (I know that when I do), it is health to my flesh and strength to my bones.

_____

_____

_____

_____

_____

Proverbs 3: 5-8

Trust in the Lord with all your heart, and lean not on your own understanding; in all your ways acknowledge Him, and He shall direct your paths. Do not be wise in your own eyes; fear the lord and depart from evil, it will be health to your flesh, and strength to your bones.

Before I knew how much He really does love me, I did not see much of a future for myself, never mind hope! Now I soak all of His promises in and I know I have hope, real hope!

Do you know this hope?

Jeremiah 29: 11-13

Dear Lord, You know the thoughts You have toward me, thoughts of peace and not of evil, to give me a future and a hope. (Thank You, Lord, for Your promises!)

I call upon You and I pray to You, and You listen to me; when I seek You, I find You when I search for You with all my heart. (Thank You so much for being there for me whenever I need You!)

_____

_____

_____

_____

Jeremiah 29:11-13

For I know the thoughts that I think toward you, says the Lord, thoughts of peace and not of evil, to give you a future and a hope.

Then you will call upon Me and go and pray to Me, and I will listen to you. And you will seek Me and find Me, when you search for Me with all your heart.

1 John 4: 7-11

Dear Lord, put in my heart love for others, because love is from You, God. Because I love, I am born of You and I know You. (I pray that I will not be resistant to love others) because when I do not love, I am not in You, God; for You are love.

Your love was manifested towards me when You, Father, gave up Your only Son, so that I might live through Him. You are the perfect example of love. I did not love You first, You loved me first. You sent Your Son for me, to take away my sin. Help me love others just as You love me. Amen.

_____

_____

_____

_____

_____

1 John 4:7-11

Beloved, let us love one another, for love is of God; and everyone who loves is born of God and knows God. He who does not love does not know God, for God is love.

In this the love of God was manifested toward us, that God has sent His only begotten son into the world, that we might live through Him.

In this is love, not that we loved God, but that He loved us and sent His son to be the propitiation of our sins. Beloved, if God so loved us, we also ought to love one another.

1 John 5: 14-15

Dear Lord, thank You for the confidence that I have in You. When I ask for anything according to Your will, I know in my heart that You hear me.

And because I know You hear me, whatever I ask for, I know You provide. (Thank You for being so gracious and seeing me for who I am.) In Your name I pray, Amen.

_____

_____

_____

_____

_____

1 John 5:14-15

Now this is the confidence that we have in Him, that if we ask anything according to His will, He hears us. And if we know that He hears us, whatever we ask, we know that we have the petitions that we have asked of Him.

Habakkuk 3:18-19

Dear Lord, I rejoice in You! I will always enjoy You, God of my salvation! You, Lord God, are my strength. (I can do nothing apart from You!)

You make my feet like the deer's feet! You enable me to walk on my high hills! I thank You, Father, Lord of heaven and earth! Amen.

_____

_____

_____

_____

_____

Habakkuk 3:18-19

Yet I will rejoice in the Lord, I will joy in the God of my salvation. The Lord God is my strength; He will make my feet like the deer's feet, and He will make me walk on my high hills.

Exodus 33:12-14

Dear Lord, You know me by name; I have found grace in Your sight.

Since I have found grace in Your sight, show me Your way, that I may know You and continue to find grace in Your sight.

Thank You that Your presence always goes with me and that You give me rest. Amen.

_____

_____

_____

_____

_____

Exodus 33:12-14

Then Moses said to the Lord, see you say to me, bring up this people. But you have not let me know whom You will send with me.

You have said, I know you by name, and You have also found grace in My sight, now therefore, I pray, if I have found grace in Your sight, show me now Your way, that I may know You and that I may find grace in Your sight.

And consider that this nation is Your people and He said, My presence will go with you, and I will give you rest.

My Accountability Before My God

**Matthew 6:19-21 | 2 Corinthians 13:3-4
Matthew 7:1-5 | Romans 6:14-23
2 Corinthians 12:7-10 | Matthew 22:37
Colossians 3:1-4**

✶✶✶✶✶

These verses and passages help me to stay humble and keep me from thinking I'm the one who keeps my life going on its course, when it has been Him arranging things the whole time!

Matthew 6:19-21

Dear Lord, I do not save for myself treasures on earth, where moth and rust destroy and someone could break in and steal. Instead help me build up treasures in heaven, where neither moth nor rust are able to destroy and where thieves cannot break in and steal.

You tell me Lord, that where my treasure is, there my heart will be also. (Give me a heart for You and for Your people. And forgive me for being so selfish so often.) Amen.

_____

_____

_____

_____

_____

Matthew 6:19-21

Do not lay up for yourselves treasures on earth, where moth and rust destroy and where thieves break in and steal; but layup yourselves treasures in heaven, where neither moth nor rust destroys and where thieves do not break in and steal. For where your treasure is, there your heart will be also.

2 Corinthians 13:3-4

Dear Lord, make me an example of strength through Your power that works in me. You were crucified in weakness, yet You live by the power of God.

I am also weak in You, yet I can live with You by the power that God has toward me. Amen!

_____

_____

_____

_____

_____

2 Corinthians 13:3-4

Since you seek a proof of Christ speaking in me, who is not weak towards you, but mighty in you. For though He was crucified in weakness, yet He lives by the power of God. For we also are weak in Him, but we shall live with Him by the power of God toward you.

I see myself so clearly in this passage. When I "help" people, I think I have so much to offer; but if I just stepped back a little I would see that I have so much junk of my own to clear out before I can even think about "helping" others!

Has this ever been an issue for you?

Matthew 7:1-5

Dear Lord, I will not judge others, because when I judge, I am judged in the same way. And the measure I use will be used against me.

Lord, I pray that I would not look at the speck in others people's eyes when I have a plank in my own eye. I pray that I would not be a hypocrite.

I will remove the plank from my eye before I try to help others with the speck in theirs.

(Thank You for teaching me this!) Amen.

_____

_____

_____

_____

Matthew 7:1-5

Judge not, that you be not judged. For with what judgment you judge, you will be judged; and with the measure you use, it will be measured back to you.

And why do you look at the speck in your brother's eye, but do not consider the plank in your own eye? Or how can you say to your brother, let me remove the speck in your eye; and look, a plank is in your own eye?

Hypocrite! First remove the plank from your own eye, and then you will see clearly to remove the speck from your brother's eye.

You and I are under grace and not bound by sin. I am always looking to Him to remind me of this.

Romans 6:14-23

I am under Your grace, and no longer am I bound by sin; sin no longer has dominion over me. Help me obey only Your Word, which leads to everlasting life! I am not under law, but under grace!

Now, having been set free from sin, I am a slave to God. I have the first fruits of Holiness, and at the end, I have eternal life.

The wages of my sin is death, but the gift of God to me is eternal life in You, Jesus Christ my Lord! Thank You, Lord God! Amen.

_____

_____

_____

_____

_____

Romans 6:14-23

For sin shall not have dominion over you, for you are not under law but under grace. What then? Shall we sin because we are not under law but under grace? Certainly not!

Do you not know that to whom you present yourselves slaves to obey, you are that one's slaves whom you obey, whether of sin leading to death, or of obedience leading to righteousness?

But God be thanked that though you were slaves of sin, yet you obeyed from the heart that form of doctrine to which you were delivered and having been set free from sin, you became slaves of righteousness.

I speak in human terms because of the weakness in your flesh. For just as you presented your members as slaves of uncleanness, and the lawlessness leading to more lawlessness, so now present your members as slaves of righteousness for Holiness.

For when you were slaves of sin, you were free in regard to righteousness. What fruit did you have in the things of which you are now ashamed? For the end of those things is death.

But now having been set free from sin, and having become slaves of God, you have your fruit to holiness and the end, everlasting life. For the wages of sin is death, but the gift of God is eternal life in Christ Jesus our Lord.

Sometimes I am frustrated with my body and the problems I have with it, but God is in control. I need to remember to be content, because He will give me the grace I need to live in this body.

2 Corinthians 12:7-10

Dear Lord, when I get full of myself, correct me with your loving discipline to bring me back to You.

You tell me that Your Grace is sufficient for me, for Your strength is made perfect in my weakness. Lord, I gladly suffer through my hardship, so that Your power is upon me.

I am content with what You have given me in my life. For when I am weak, then I am strongest in You. (I give You the glory when I am strong in You!)

_____

_____

_____

_____

_____

2 Corinthians 12:7-10

And lest I should be exalted above measure by the abundance of the revelations, a thorn in the flesh was given to me, a messenger of Satan to buffet me, lest I be exalted above measure.

Concerning this thing I pleaded with the Lord three times that it might depart from me. And He said to me, My grace is sufficient for you, for My strength is made perfect in weakness.

Therefore most gladly I would rather boast in my infirmities, that the power of Christ may rest upon me. Therefore I take pleasure in infirmities, in reproaches, in needs, in persecutions, in distresses, for Christ's sake.

For when I am weak then I am strong.

Matthew 22:37

I love You, my God, with all my heart, with all my soul, and with all my mind.

(I pray for Your strength to help me focus on what You want with my entire being.) Amen.

_____

_____

_____

_____

_____

Matthew 22:37

Jesus said to him, you shall love the Lord your God with all your heart, with all your soul, and with all your mind.

Colossians 3:1-4

Dear Father in heaven, thank You for saving me and raising me with Your Son. I seek things which are above, where Christ my Lord sits at the right hand of our Father.

I set my mind on things above, not on things on the earth, because my old life is dead and now I am hidden with You, Lord Jesus, and with God our father! You are my life. When You appear, I will be with You in glory!

Thank You for Your promises, Lord! Amen!

_____

_____

_____

_____

_____

Colossians 3:1-4

If then you were raised with Christ, seek those things which are above, where Christ is, sitting at the right hand of God. Set your mind on things above, not on things on the earth.

For you died, and your life is hidden with Christ in God. When Christ who is our life appears, then you also will appear with Him in glory.

Seeking Your Forgiveness

**1 Timothy 6:11-13 | Isaiah 55:6-12 | Micah 7:18-
20   Matthew 6:9-15 | Romans 7:14-18
2 Corinthians 5:14-21 | Colossians 1:21-23
Titus 3:2-8 | Hebrews 4:14-16 | Ephesians 5:8-10
1 John 1:9 | James 4:7-8**

*****

I am always trying to do things on my own and in my own way!
I stumble so many times, yet I never get the hint.

Whenever I am living in my own power, I am apart from Him
and His power, and my life doesn't work quite right! These
verses bring me back down from myself and into Him!

1 Timothy 6:11-13

Because I am Your child, I flee evil things and pursue righteousness, godliness, faith, love, patience, and gentleness.

(In Your strength) I fight the good fight of faith, and I lay hold of the eternal life to which I was called and which I confess before many witnesses. I praise You, God, who gives life to all things. Amen.

_____

_____

_____

_____

_____

1 Timothy 6:11-13

But you, O man of God, flee these things and pursue righteousness, godliness, faith, love, patience, gentleness. Fight the good fight of faith, lay hold on eternal life, to which you were called and have confessed the good confession in the presence of many witnesses.

I urge you in the sight of God who gives life to all things, and before Christ Jesus who witnessed the good confession before Pontius Pilate...

Isaiah 55:6-12

I seek You while You can still be found. I call upon You while You are near, and when I am wicked and forsake Your way and am unrighteous in my thoughts, I return to You, Lord, and You have mercy on me; and to You, God, for You abundantly pardon and forgive me.

My God, Your thoughts are not my thoughts nor are Your ways my ways! As the heavens are higher than the earth, so are Your ways higher than my ways and Your thoughts higher than mine!

Your words are true when they come out of Your mouth; and they do not come back empty, but accomplish whatever You please and prosper in what You sent them for. I go out with joy and I am led out with peace.

The mountains and the hills shall break forth into singing before You and the trees of the field will clap their hands! Amen!

_____

_____

_____

_____

_____

Isaiah 55:6-12

Seek the Lord while He may be found, call upon Him while He is near.

Let the wicked forsake his way, and the unrighteous man his thoughts; let him return to the Lord, and He will have mercy on him; and to our God, for He will abundantly pardon, for My thoughts are not your thoughts, nor are your ways My ways, says the Lord.

For as the heavens are higher than the earth, so are My ways higher than your ways, and My thoughts higher than your thoughts.

For as the rain comes down and the snow from heaven and do not return there, but water the earth, and make it bring forth the bud, that it may give seed to the sower and bread to the eater,

so shall My word be that goes forth from My mouth: it shall not return to Me void, but it shall accomplish what I please, and it shall prosper in the thing for which I sent it.

For you shall go out with joy, and be led out with peace: the mountains and the hills shall break forth into singing before You and all the trees of the field shall clap their hands.

This is a great verse that I meditate on when I need to get right with God. He's so merciful!

How does this make you feel when you read it? Do you ever need to be reminded of how much you are forgiven?

Micah 7:18-20

There is no other God like You, who pardons my sin and forgives my transgressions! I thank You for Your promise that You do not stay angry with me forever, but You delight in mercy!

You have compassion on me and subdue my iniquities. You cast my sins into the depths of the sea! Thank You for being so merciful! You are and will be the same, today, tomorrow and always!

(I rejoice in the fact that I am Your child, and I am covered by Your sacrifice! I am truly blessed to be Your child!) Amen!

_____

_____

_____

_____

_____

Micah 7:18-20

Who is a God like You, pardoning iniquity and passing over the transgression of the remnant of His heritage? He does not retain His anger forever, because He delights in mercy. He will again have compassion on us, and will subdue our iniquities. You will cast all our sins into the depths of the sea. You will give truth to Jacob and mercy to Abraham, which You have sworn to our fathers from days of old.

This is a familiar passage. Do you notice a difference when you read it in first person?

Matthew 6:9-15

My Father in Heaven, Holy is Your name! I look for Your kingdom to come soon, and I pray that Your will is done on earth as it is in heaven.

Give me my portion, my Lord, enough for today. Forgive my sins as I forgive those who sin against me. And do not lead me into temptation, but deliver me from the evil one.

For Yours is the kingdom, the power, and the glory forever! Amen.

When I forgive others then you will forgive me, but when I am unforgiving you do not forgive me.

_____

_____

_____

_____

_____

Matthew 6:9-15

In this manner, therefore, pray: Our father in heaven, hallowed be Your name. Your kingdom come. Your will be done on earth as it is in heaven. Give us this day our daily bread.

And forgive us our debts, as we forgive our debtors. And do not lead us into temptation, but deliver us from the evil one. For Yours is the kingdom and the power and the glory forever. Amen.

For if you forgive men their trespasses, your heavenly Father will also forgive you. But if you do not forgive men their trespasses, neither will your Father forgive your trespasses.

This verse keeps me aware how much I really do sin, every day. I use it as a great foundation for prayer to ask Him for forgiveness.

Do you see yourself here too?

Romans 7:14-18

Dear Lord, I am a sinner. I do not understand the things I do. The things I want to do, I do not do, but what I hate, that is what I do.

But if I do what I do not want to do, it's no longer I, but the sin living in me. Good does not dwell in my natural self. I am sinful by nature, for I have the desire to do what is good, but I cannot do it.

(Forgive me when I sin in my weakness. Lead me with Your strength and wisdom to do what is right in Your eyes, and forgive me for sinning in Your sight.

Thank You for restoring me to You! In Jesus' name! Amen!)

_____

_____

_____

_____

_____

Romans 7:14-18

For we know that the law is spiritual, but I am carnal, sold under sin. For what I am doing, I do not understand. For what I will to do, that I do not practice; but what I hate, that I do.

If, then, I do what I will not to do, I agree with the law that it is good. But now, it is no longer I who do it, but sin that dwells in me.

For I know that in me (that is, in my flesh) nothing good dwells; for to will is present with me, but how to perform what is good I do not find.

This passage reminds me that I was saved when Jesus died for me. He paid it all and there is nothing left! He said, "It is finished." This makes me truly forgiven and closer to Him than ever!

2 Corinthians 5:14-21

The love You have for me compels me. I am convicted and fully convinced that You died for me and my sin; so I must die to them also. I know that my sins died on the cross with You.

Since You died for me, I should not live for myself, but for You, Lord, who died for me and was raised again. I pray now that I will be able to see things through Your eyes. Because I am in You, my Lord Jesus, I am a new creation; the old one is gone!

Thank You, Lord, for reconciling me to Yourself and for not counting my sins against me. Make me a good witness and useful to bring others to You, God. Your Father made You, my Lord, who had no sin, to die for my sin so that in You I would become righteous in Your sight!

Thank You, gracious Father. Amen.

_____

_____

_____

_____

2 Corinthians 5:14-21

For the love of Christ compels us, because we judge thus: that if One died for all, then all died; and He died for all, that those who live should live no longer for themselves, but for Him who died for them and rose again.

Therefore, from now on, we regard no one according to the flesh. Even though we have known Christ according to the flesh, yet now we know Him thus no longer. Therefore, if anyone is in Christ, he is a new creation; old things have passed away; behold, all things have become new.

Now all things are of God, who has reconciled us to Himself through Jesus Christ, and has given us the ministry of reconciliation, that is, that God was in Christ reconciling the world to Himself, not imputing their trespasses to them, and has committed to us the word of reconciliation.

Now then, we are ambassadors for Christ, as though God were pleading through us: we implore you on Christ's behalf, be reconciled to God. For He made Him who knew no sin to be sin for us, that I might become the righteousness of God in Him.

Colossians 1:21-23

Dear Lord, (thank You for already forgiving me). I was once alienated and an enemy of Yours by my thoughts and deeds; yet You reconciled me to Yourself. You died for me.

Now I am presented holy and blameless and above reproach in Your sight! I pray that I will continue in my faith, grounded and steadfast.

I pray that I am not moved away from the hope of the Gospel that I learned, and that was preached to every creature under heaven.

(I, too, want to share it with everyone! Give me the courage to do that, Lord! In Jesus' name, Amen.)

_____

_____

_____

_____

_____

Colossians 1:21-23

And you, who were once alienated and enemies in your mind by wicked works, yet now He has reconciled in the body of His flesh through death, to present you holy, and blameless, and above reproach in His sight-

if indeed you continue in the faith, grounded and steadfast, and are not moved away from the hope of the gospel which you heard, which was preached to every creature under heaven, of which I, Paul, became a minister.

Titus 3:2-8

Dear Father, (since I have Your love in me), I do not speak evil of anyone; I am peaceable and gentle; and I am humble in all things.

Without You, I am foolish and disobedient, I am easily deceived, I serve all kinds of lusts and pleasures, and without You I live in malice and envy. I'm hateful and I hate others.

I thank You for the love and kindness You give to me. It wasn't anything I did; but because of Your mercy, You washed me and regenerated me with the renewing of Your Holy Spirit whom You poured out on me abundantly through Your Son, Jesus Christ, my Savior!

Now I am justified by Your grace. Now I am an heir according to the hope that is eternal life, because I believe in You, God. I know now that I am ready to do good works to profit Your people. Thank You that Your grace is in me always. In Jesus' name, amen.

_____

_____

_____

_____

_____

Titus 3:2-8

Put them in mind to speak evil of no one, to be peaceable, gentle, showing all humility to all men. For we ourselves were also once foolish, disobedient, deceived, serving various lusts and pleasures, living in malice and envy, hateful and hating one another.

But when the kindness and the love of God our Savior toward man appeared, not by works of righteousness which we have done, but according to His mercy He saved us, through the washing of regeneration and renewing of the Holy Spirit,

whom He poured out on us abundantly through Jesus Christ our savior, that having been justified by His grace we should become heirs according to the hope of eternal life.

This is a faithful saying, and these things I want you to affirm constantly, that those who have believed in God should be careful to maintain good works. These things are good and profitable to men.

This passage helps me to understand how perfect He really is, and how He knew then, and knows now, how hard it is for us to walk in this life, because He lived it Himself! He knows how weak I am, and He saved me anyway!

Doesn't it make you, too, feel special?!

Hebrews 4:14-16

Dear Lord, You are my great high priest. You have passed through the heavens, Jesus, son of God! I confess my sins to You.

You are my High Priest and can sympathize with me in my weakness, because when You were tempted in every way, You did not sin.

Because of this, I come boldly to Your throne of grace and I obtain mercy and find Your grace to help me in my time of need!

(Thank you, Father, that in my time of need, You hear me and answer my prayers before I even ask!) Amen.

_____

_____

_____

_____

_____

Hebrews 4:14-16

Seeing then that we have a great High Priest who has passed through the heavens, Jesus the Son of God, let us hold fast our confession.

For we do not have a High Priest who cannot sympathize with our weaknesses, but was in all points tempted as we are, yet without sin.

Let us therefore come boldly to the throne of grace that we may obtain mercy and find grace to help in time of need.

Ephesians 5:8-10

I was in darkness. (Thank You), Lord, for filling me with Your light! Now I live as a child of that light, and I bear the fruit of the Spirit that light brings.

(I have Your goodness, righteousness, and truth in me), and I pray that I will keep finding out what pleases You! In Your name, I pray, amen.

_____

_____

_____

_____

_____

Ephesians 5:8-10

For you were once darkness, but now you are light in the Lord. Walk as children of light (for the fruit of the spirit is in all goodness, righteousness, and truth), finding out what is acceptable to the Lord.

This is the classic "forgive me" verse. Short and to the point. This reminds me just how merciful He really is.

1 John 1:9

When I confess my sins, You are faithful and just to forgive my sins and cleanse me of all unrighteousness!

(You are my wonderful Savior! Thank You for Your grace and mercy. Amen!)

_____

_____

_____

_____

_____

1 John 1:9

If we confess our sins, He is faithful and just to forgive us our sins and to cleanse us from all unrighteousness.

James 4:7-8

Father in heaven, I submit to You, my Lord, every day. As I resist the devil, he flees from me. Thank You that whenever I draw near to You, Lord, You draw near to me!

Give me clean hands and a pure heart and make me never double minded. (God, please work in me and through me.) Amen!

_____

_____

_____

_____

_____

James 4:7-8

Therefore submit to God. Resist the devil and he will flee from you. Draw near to God and he will draw near to you.

Cleanse your hands, you sinners; and purify your hearts, you double minded.

When I Am Going Through Pain or Fear

**Acts 2:25-28 | 1 John 4:17-19 | Deuteronomy 31:6
Psalm 34:4-9 | Romans 8:18-23 | 2 Timothy 1:7-9
Psalm 27:4-5**

*****

In my life, I am in (physical) pain a lot, and it makes me fearful of the future sometimes. These verses and passages help me to see that this physical life is not all there is.

Acts 2:25-28

(Peter, quoting Psalm 16:8-11)

Dear Lord, I always see You before me. You are at my right hand. I will not be shaken; therefore, my heart is glad and my tongue rejoices! I pray that my body will also rest in hope.

You will not abandon me to the realm of the dead! Nor will You let Your Holy One see decay! You have made known to me the paths of life; fill me with joy in Your presence always! Amen.

_____

_____

_____

_____

_____

Acts 2: 25-28

I foresaw the Lord always before my face, for He is at my right hand, that I may not be shaken. Therefore my heart rejoiced, and my tongue was glad;

moreover my flesh also will rest in hope. For you will not leave my soul in Hades, nor will You allow Your Holy One to see corruption. You have made known to me the ways of life;

You will make me full of joy in your presence.

1 John 4:17-19

Love has been perfected in me in this: that I will have boldness in the Day of Judgment because as You are, so am I in this world.

I do not fear, because there is no fear in love. Perfect love casts out fear. If I fear, I am not in You, Lord. I love You, Lord, because You first loved me! Amen!

_____

_____

_____

_____

_____

1 John 4:17-19

Love has been perfected among us in this: that we may have boldness in the Day of Judgment; because as He is, so are we in this world,

there is no fear in love; but perfect love casts out fear, because fear involves torment.

But he who fears has not been made perfect in love. For we love Him because He first loved us.

This next verse is so comforting to me, and I feel that it could fit in many sections of this book. I like to come to this one when I'm feeling afraid or am in pain.

It says so much about His present-ness in my life. "He goes with me." Even when people let me down, I know He's always there.

Has this verse ever been helpful to you in your life?

Deuteronomy 31:6

Father in heaven, I am strong and of good courage. I do not fear and I am not afraid, for You, Lord, go with me.

You will never leave me or forsake me.

(Thank You for Your glorious promises!)

_____

_____

_____

_____

_____

Deuteronomy 31:6

Be strong and of good courage, do not fear nor be afraid of them: for the Lord your God, He is the One who goes with you. He will not leave you nor forsake you.

Psalm 34:4-9

Dear Lord, because I seek You, You hear me and deliver me from all my fears. Thank You that when I look to You, I am radiant and You will see no shame in me.

(Oh Lord), when I cry out to You, You hear me and save me from all of my troubles! Your angels are all around and they guard me because they know that I fear You, (my King)!

Oh, I have tasted and seen that You, Lord, are good, and I am blessed because I trust in You! There is nothing I need aside from You (and what You want me to have). In Your precious name, Amen.

_____

_____

_____

_____

_____

Psalm 34:4-9

I sought the Lord, and He heard me, and delivered me from all my fears. They looked to Him and were radiant, and their faces were not ashamed.

This poor man cried out, and the Lord heard him, and saved him out of all his troubles. The angel of the Lord encamps all around those who fear Him, and delivers them.

Oh, taste and see that the Lord is good; blessed is the man who trusts in Him!

O fear the Lord, you his saints! There is no want to those who fear Him.

Romans 8:18-23

Dear Lord, I consider the sufferings I am going through today not worthy to be compared with the glory which shall be revealed in me when I go home to You.

Through Your will, I am set free from the slavery of my flesh into the freedom that belongs to a child of God. I know the whole creation groans and suffers until now.

Even I, having the fruits of the Spirit, still groan within myself, waiting eagerly for the redemption of my body. (I look forward to Your promises!) Amen!

_____

_____

_____

_____

_____

Romans 8:18-23

For I consider that the sufferings of this present time are not worthy to be compared with the glory which shall be revealed in us for the earnest expectation of the creation eagerly awaits for the revealing of the sons of God.

For the creation was subjected to futility, not willingly, but because of Him who subjected it in hope, because the creation itself also will be delivered from the bondage of corruption into the glorious liberty of the children of God.

For we know that the whole creation groans and labors with birth pangs together until now. Not only that, but we also who have the first fruits of the spirit, even we ourselves groan within ourselves, eagerly waiting for the adoption, the redemption of the body.

This verse gives me so much confidence in myself by knowing that He has not given me a spirit of fear, but of power and love and sound mind!

Do you know He has given all this to you too?

2 Timothy 1:7-9

Dear Lord, (whenever I am afraid, I meditate on these words): You have not given me the spirit of fear, but of power and of love and of a sound mind. I will not be ashamed of Your testimony.

You saved me and called me with a holy calling, not according to my works, but for Your own purpose and grace, which was given to me in Christ Jesus before time began! In Your name I pray, Amen.

_____

_____

_____

_____

_____

2 Timothy 1:7-9

For God has not given us a spirit of fear, but of power and of love and of a sound mind. Therefore, do not be ashamed of the testimony of our Lord, nor of me his prisoner,

but share with me in the sufferings for the gospel according to the power of God who has saved us and called us with a holy calling,

not according to our works, but according to His own purpose and grace which was given to us in Christ Jesus for time began.

Psalm 27:4-5

Dear Lord, I desire You in my heart. I seek only You. Let me dwell in Your house, Lord, all the days of my life to see Your beauty!

In times of trouble, I will call on You, and You will hear me. You will hide me in Your pavilion and in the secret place of Your tabernacle. You will set me high upon a rock! In Your name I pray, amen.

_____

_____

_____

_____

_____

Psalm 27:4-5

One thing I have desired of the Lord, that I will seek: That I may dwell in the house of the Lord all the days of my life, to behold the beauty of the Lord, and to inquire in His temple.

For in the time of trouble He shall hide me in His pavilion; In the secret place of His tabernacle He shall hide me: He shall set me high upon a rock.

Praying Through Trials and Tribulations

Psalm 121:1-8 | Philippians 4:6-9 | James 1:2-8
1 Peter 1:3-6 | 2 Peter 1:5-8 | James 1:12
Matthew 5:43-48 | John 11:25-26

*****

Often, when I am going through hard times, it is not easy to see God's hand in my life. It really helps me to see Him more clearly when I read and pray to Him. Some of these verses and passages help me during these times.

This passage is special to me because when I read it, it helps me see that He really is everywhere! He is with me all the time! He wants me to look for Him!

Psalm 121:1-8

When I need help, I lift my eyes to the hills and look for You, where my help comes from.

You are maker of heaven and earth! You do not allow my foot to slip. You neither sleep nor slumber! Lord, You are the shade at my right hand; the sun will not overtake me by day nor the moon at night!

You, Lord, preserve my soul from all evil. You watch me when I come in and when I go out. (I praise You, God, from this time forth and forever!) Amen!

_____

_____

_____

_____

_____

Psalm 121:1-8

I will lift up my eyes to the hills – from whence comes my help? My help comes from the Lord, who made heaven and earth. He will not allow your foot to be moved;

He who keeps you will not slumber. Behold, He who keeps Israel shall neither sleep nor slumber. Shall neither slumber nor sleep. The Lord is your keeper; the Lord is your shade at your right hand.

The sun shall not strike you by day, nor the moon by night. The Lord shall preserve you from all evil; He shall preserve your soul. The Lord shall preserve your going out and your coming in from this time forth, and even forevermore.

This passage helps me to focus on what really is important in my day and reminds me that there's no room for worry.

Philippians 4:6-9

Dear Lord, I am not anxious; but in everything, by prayer and supplication, with thanksgiving, I make my requests known to You, God. I pray that Your peace, my God, which surpasses all understanding, guards my heart and mind.

I meditate on whatever things are true, noble, and just, whatever things are pure, lovely, and of good report. If there is any virtue, if there is anything praiseworthy, I meditate on these things.

And I pray that all the things which I have learned and received and heard and seen in You, Lord, I do. When I do these things, Your peace is in me and with me! In Your name I pray, amen!

_____

_____

_____

_____

_____

Philippians 4:6-9

Be anxious for nothing, but everything by prayer and supplication, with thanksgiving, let your requests be made known to God; and the peace of God, which surpasses all understanding, will guard your hearts and minds through Christ Jesus.

Finally, brethren, whatever things are true, whatever things are noble, whatever things are just, whatever things are pure, whatever things are lovely, whatever things are of good report, if there is any virtue and if there is anything praiseworthy-meditate on these things.

The things which you learned and received and heard and saw in me, these do, and the God of peace will be with you.

This passage helps me to remember that when I'm going through trials, He's still there with me and He wants me to get even stronger and to trust Him no matter what!

James 1:2-8

I consider it joy whenever I am faced with trials, because I know that when my faith is tested, I grow in patience, and as patience does its perfect work, I will become complete and perfect in You, Lord, lacking nothing.

If I lack wisdom, I ask You, God, because when I ask You in faith, You give to me generously. And when I ask You for something in faith, I do not doubt, but believe that You have done it for me already, before I even ask.

I know that I receive whatever I ask when I trust You and do not doubt; but if I pray doubting, I would be like someone who is on a wave in the sea, blown to and fro. I can never expect to receive anything from You when I doubt, because I am a double minded person, unstable in all I do.

_____

_____

_____

_____

_____

James 1:2-8

My brethren, count it all joy when you fall into various trials, knowing that the testing of your faith produces patience. But let patience have its perfect work, that you may be perfect and complete, lacking nothing.

If any of you lacks wisdom, let him ask of God, who gives to all liberally and without reproach, and it will be given to him. But let him ask in faith, with no doubting, for he who doubts is like a wave of the sea driven and tossed by the wind.

For let not that man supposes that he will receive anything from the Lord; he is a double minded man, unstable and all his ways.

1 Peter 1:3-6

I bless You, God, and thank You, Father, that according to Your abundant mercy, You give me new birth into a living hope through Jesus, who is resurrected from the dead.

I thank You that You bring me into a perfect inheritance that can never perish, spoil, or fade, and that this inheritance is kept in heaven for me. I thank You that I am kept by Your power through faith for the salvation that is reserved for me.

In all this I greatly rejoice! I will keep these words close to my heart, even now when I am going through trials.

_____

_____

_____

_____

_____

1 Peter 1:3-6

Blessed be the God and father of our Lord Jesus Christ, who according to His abundant mercy has begotten us again to a living hope through the resurrection of Jesus Christ from the dead,

to an inheritance incorruptible and undefiled that does not fade away, reserved in heaven for you, who are kept by the power of God through faith for salvation ready to be revealed in the last time.

In this you greatly rejoice, though now for a little while, if need be, you have been grieved by various trials.

2 Peter 1:5-8

Dear Lord, through the faith You have given to me, and with Your strength, I make every effort to add to my faith, goodness; and to my goodness, knowledge; and to my knowledge, self-control; and to my self-control, perseverance; and to my perseverance, godliness; and to my godliness, mutual affection; and to my mutual affection, love.

I pray that I would possess these qualities in increasing measure; and as they grow in my life, they will help keep me growing in effective and productive fruitfulness in my knowledge of You, my Lord. (Thank You for Your words and promises.) Amen.

_____

_____

_____

_____

_____

2 Peter 1:5-8

But also for this very reason, giving all diligence, add to your faith virtue, to virtue knowledge, to knowledge self-control, to self-control perseverance, to perseverance godliness, to godliness brotherly kindness, and to brotherly kindness love.

For if these things are yours and abound, you will be neither barren nor unfruitful in the knowledge of our Lord Jesus Christ.

James 1:12

Dear Lord, bless me when I am tempted. Because when I endure, then I will be approved and receive the crown of life that You, my Lord, have promised to me, because I love You (and You love me, my Savior).

(To You be the glory, both now and forever.) Amen.

_____

_____

_____

_____

_____

James 1:12

Blessed is the man who endures temptation; for when he has been approved, he will receive the crown of life which the Lord has promised to those who love Him.

Matthew 5:43-48

I have heard people say that I am to love my neighbor and hate my enemy.

But because You tell me to, Lord, I love my enemies, I bless those who curse me, I do good to those who hate me, and I pray for those who spitefully use me and persecute me, because I am Your child, my Father in Heaven.

_____

_____

_____

_____

_____

Matthew 5:43-48

You have heard it said, you shall love your neighbor and hate your enemy. But I say to you, love your enemies, bless those who curse you, do good to those who hate you, and pray for those who spitefully use you and persecute you, that you may be sons of your Father in heaven.

Do you believe this?

John 11:25-26

You are the resurrection and the life. (You are my resurrection and my life!) Because I believe in You, even though my body will die, I will live. Because I live and believe in You, I will never die! (Thank you, Jesus!) Amen.

_____

_____

_____

_____

_____

John 11:25-26

Jesus said to her, I am the resurrection and the life. He who believes in me, though he may die, he shall live. And whoever lives and believes in me shall never die.

When I Need Comfort In You, God

Psalm 29:1-4 | Psalm 23 | Psalm 48:14 | Isaiah 46:4   Psalm 121:1-8 | Matthew 5:3-9 | Matthew 6:25-34   Matthew 11:28-30 | Philippians 4:4-7 Philippians 4:11-13 | Deuteronomy 31:6 Hebrews 13:20-21 | Nahum 1:7

*****

When I am sad or depressed, these verses and passages bring me right back to His face; He is so wonderful to me! The clouds may be here right now, but I know the sun will shine soon. I just need to wait!

Psalm 29:1-4

I will praise You with all that is in me! Glory and strength belong to Your name! You are glorious! I give You the glory due to Your name when I worship You in the splendor of Your Holiness.

Your voice is over the waters! I hear Your glory when You thunder over the waters! Your voice is powerful! Your voice is majestic! (I will give praise to You, Most High! You are the mighty God I love! Amen!)

_____

_____

_____

_____

_____

Psalm 29: 1-4

Give unto the Lord, O you mighty ones; give unto the Lord glory and strength. Give unto the Lord the glory due to His name; worship the Lord in the beauty of holiness. The voice of the Lord is over the waters; the God of glory thunders; the Lord is over many waters. The voice of the Lord is powerful; the voice of the Lord is full of majesty.

This passage is already in first person, but I love it so much, I couldn't resist putting it in!

Psalm 23

You, Lord, are my shepherd. I shall not want. You make me lie down in green pastures. You lead me beside the still waters. You restore my soul; You lead me in the paths of righteousness for Your name's sake.

Even when I walk through the valley of the shadow of death, I fear no evil, because You are with me; Your rod and Your staff, they comfort me. You prepare a table before me in the presence of my enemies. You anoint my head with oil. My cup runs over.

Surely goodness and mercy shall follow me all the days of my life, and I will dwell in Your house, Lord, forever. Amen!

_____

_____

_____

_____

Psalm 23

The Lord is my shepherd; I shall not want. He makes me to lie down in green pastures; He leads me beside the still waters. He restores my soul; He leads me in the paths of righteousness for His name's sake.

Yea, though I walk through the valley of the shadow of death, I will fear no evil; for You are with me; Your rod and Your staff, they comfort me. You prepare a table before me in the presence of my enemies; You anoint my head with oil; my cup runs over.

Surely goodness and mercy shall follow me all the days of my life; and I will dwell in the house of the Lord forever.

Psalm 48:14

You are my God forever and ever. You are my guide even unto death!

(Therefore, I do not fear death! I look forward to being with You in Your kingdom!)

_____

_____

_____

_____

_____

Psalm 48:14

For this is God, our God forever and ever; He will be our guide even to death…

Isaiah 46:4

You will be my God throughout my lifetime, until my hair is white with age. You made me and You will care for me! You carry me along this life and keep me safe!

_____

_____

_____

_____

_____

Isaiah 46:4

Even to your old age, I am He, and even to gray hairs I will carry you! I have made, and will bear; even I will carry, and will deliver you.

This passage is in this book twice because I thought that it fit so well into this category as well as in the trials and tribulations category. It always comforts me and in the past, it has helped me to get through some pretty tough times!

Psalm 121:1-8

When I need help, I lift my eyes to the hills and look for You, where my help comes from. You are the maker of heaven and earth! You will not allow my foot to slip.

You neither sleep nor slumber! Lord, You are my keeper, You are the shade at my right hand; the sun will not overtake me by day nor the moon at night!

You, Lord, will preserve my soul from all evil. You watch me when I come in and when I go out. (I will praise You, God,) from now until forever! Amen!

_____

_____

_____

_____

_____

Psalm 121:1-8

I will lift up my eyes to the hills – from whence comes my help? My help comes from the Lord, who made heaven and earth. He will not allow your foot to be moved; He who keeps you will not slumber.

Behold, He who keeps Israel shall neither sleep nor slumber. Shall neither slumber nor sleep. The Lord is your keeper; the Lord is your shade at your right hand. The sun shall not strike you by day, nor the moon by night.

The Lord shall preserve you from all evil; He shall preserve your soul. The Lord shall preserve your going out and you're coming in from this time forth, and even forevermore.

The following verses assure me that He covers every part of my life. No matter where I am in life, He understands and takes care of me.

How does this passage sound when you read it with you in it?

Matthew 5:3-9

When I am poor in spirit, You bless me with the kingdom of heaven. When I mourn, You comfort me. When I am meek, You bless me with the promise of an inheritance.

When I hunger and thirst for Your righteousness, You fill me up. When I am merciful, You are merciful to me. When I am pure in my heart, I see you!

When I am peaceful, You bless me as Your child.

_____

_____

_____

_____

_____

Matthew 5:3-9

Blessed are the poor in spirit, theirs is the kingdom of heaven. Blessed are those who mourn, for they shall be comforted. Blessed are the meek, for they shall inherit the earth.

Blessed are those who hunger and thirst for righteousness, for they shall be filled. Blessed are the merciful, for they shall obtain mercy. Blessed are the pure in heart, for they shall see God.

Blessed are the peacemakers, for they shall be called sons of God.

Matthew 6:25-34

I no longer worry about my life, what I will eat or what I will drink or about my body and what I will wear. Life is more than food and my body more than clothing.

I look at the birds of the air, how they neither sow nor reap nor gather into barns; yet You, Lord, feed them. I am of so much more value than they are!

Does worrying add more height to my stature? So I do not worry about clothes. When I look and see the lilies of the field and how they grow, they neither toil nor spin and yet even Solomon in all his glory was not arrayed like one of those!

Oh Lord, You clothe the grass of the fields which today is and tomorrow is thrown into the fire. How can I, by worrying, add more than You do for me?

I know You have much better in mind for me! I no longer worry about what I'll eat or drink. Everyone needs these things, and You know I need them too.

I seek Your kingdom and Your righteousness and when I do, all those other things are given to me. So I will not worry about tomorrow. Tomorrow will worry about itself; it has its own trouble.

(Thank You for caring about every little thing, my Lord.)

_____

_____

_____

_____

_____

Matthew 6:25-34

Therefore I say to you, do not worry about your life, what you will eat or what you will drink; nor about your body, what you will put on. Is not life more than food and the body more than clothing?

Look at the birds of the air, for they neither sow nor reap nor gather into barns; yet your heavenly Father feeds them. Are you not of much more value than they? Which of you by worrying can add one cubic to his stature? So why do you worry about clothing?

Consider the lilies of the field, how they grow: they neither toil nor spin; and yet I say to you that even Solomon in all his glory was not arrayed like one of these.

Now if God so clothes the grass of the field, which today is, and tomorrow is thrown into the oven, will he not much more clothe you, O you of little faith?

Therefore do not worry, saying what shall we eat? Or what shall we drink? Or what shall we wear? For after all these things the Gentiles seek. For your heavenly father knows that you need all these things.

But seek first the kingdom of God and his righteousness and all these things shall be added to you. Therefore do not worry about tomorrow, for tomorrow will worry about its own things.

Sufficient for the day is its own trouble.

Matthew 11:28-30

When I am weary and burdened, I will come to You and You will give me rest. I will obey You and learn from You.

You are gentle and humble in heart and You will give me rest in my soul, because Your yoke is easy and Your burdens are light.

_____

_____

_____

_____

_____

Matthew 11:28-30

Come to me, all you who labor and are heavy laden, and I will give you rest. Take My yoke upon you and learn from Me, I am gentle and lowly in heart, and you will find rest for your souls.

For My yoke is easy and My burden is light.

His ways transcend all understanding! He is so present in our lives. When I look around, I see that He thought of every little thing! I will rejoice in Him always!

Have you ever considered that He actually guards your heart and mind?

Philippians 4:4-7

I rejoice in You always and my gentleness is evident to all because of You. (I wasn't always so gentle. Thank You, my Father.)

Because You are near me, I am not anxious about anything; but in every situation, by prayer and petition, with thanksgiving, I present my requests to You.

And Your peace, which transcends all understanding, guards my heart and mind through You, Lord. Amen!

_____

_____

_____

_____

_____

Philippians 4:4-7

Rejoice in the Lord always. Again I will say, rejoice! Let your gentleness be known to all men. The Lord is at hand.

Be anxious for nothing, but in everything by prayer and supplication, with thanksgiving, let your requests be made known to God;

and the peace of God, which surpasses all understanding, will guard your hearts and minds through Christ Jesus.

Philippians 4:11-13

Dear Lord, whatever state I am in, help me be content. Teach me to be content whether I have nothing or have an overabundance, whether I am hungry or full.

I can do all things through You, my Lord Jesus. You strengthen me. (Thank You for giving me this strength!) Amen.

_____

_____

_____

_____

_____

Philippians 4:11-13

Not that I speak in regard of need, for I have learned in whatsoever state I am, to be content: I know how to be abased, and I know how to abound.

Everywhere and in all things I have learned both to be full and to be hungry, both to abound and to suffer need. I can do all things through Christ who strengthens me.

Deuteronomy 31:6

(Thank You for loving me so much, and for these words:) "Be strong and of good courage. Do not be afraid." For You, Lord, will go with me. You will not leave me nor forsake me, Lord.

(You are the One who stays with me. You will not leave me nor forsake me, so I will not fear nor be dismayed. Thank You for Your glorious promises!)

_____

_____

_____

_____

_____

Deuteronomy 31:6

Be strong enough good courage, do not fear nor be afraid of them: for the Lord your God, He is the One who goes with you. He will not leave you nor forsake you.

Hebrews 13:20-21

Dear Lord, I pray for Your peace, the peace of the God who brought You, my King, up from the dead. You are my great Shepherd, and I am Your sheep. Through Your blood, You made a covenant with me.

Make me complete in every good work, that I finish the work You want me to do, that I follow Your will, and that I am pleasing in Your sight. To You, Jesus Christ, be the glory forever and ever. Amen.

_____

_____

_____

_____

_____

Hebrews 13:20-21

Now may the God of peace who brought up our Lord Jesus from the dead, that great Shepherd of the sheep, through the blood of the everlasting covenant, make you complete in every good work to do His will,

working in you what is well pleasing in His sight, through Jesus Christ, to whom be glory forever and ever, amen.

Nahum 1:7

Dear Father in heaven, You are good. You are my refuge in times of trouble. You know me and care for me, because I trust in You.

(I pray that when I am tested, I would go to You and not try to fix it myself. Thank you, Lord, for Your comforting words!) Amen.

_____

_____

_____

_____

_____

Nahum 1:7

The Lord is good, a stronghold in the day of trouble; and He knows those who trust in Him.

Praises

**Exodus 15:2 | 1 Chronicles 29:10-13
Nehemiah 9:5b-6 | Psalm 62:5-8 | Psalm 84:10-12
Isaiah 12:1-6 | Isaiah 42:5b-6 | Isaiah 60:19-21
Romans 8:24-29 | Ephesians 5:18-20 | Hebrews
11:6   Isaiah 45:22 | Deuteronomy 32:3-4
Revelation 21:3-5**

*****

Let's end this book with praises and songs! He is so wonderful; I want to yell His name from the rooftops! Thank you, Lord, for being with me wherever I go!

Exodus 15:2

You, Lord, are my strength and song. You are my salvation; You are my God, and I praise You!

_____

_____

_____

_____

_____

Exodus 15:2

The Lord is my strength and song, and He has become my salvation; He is my God, and I will praise Him.

1 Chronicles 29:10-13

Blessed are You, Lord God of Israel, my Father forever and ever! Oh Lord, Yours is the greatness, the power and the glory, the victory and the majesty.

All that is in heaven and on earth is Yours; Yours is the kingdom and You are exalted as head over all!

Both the riches and honor come from You and You reign over all. In Your hand is power and might!

By Your hand, You make great and give strength to all.

(I thank You, my God, and praise Your glorious name!)

_____

_____

_____

_____

_____

1 Chronicles 29:10-13

Therefore David blessed the Lord before all the assembly; and David said: Blessed are You, Lord God of Israel, our father forever and ever.

Yours, oh Lord, is the greatness, the power and the glory, the victory and the majesty, for all that is in heaven and in earth is Yours; Yours is the kingdom, O Lord, and You are exalted as head over all.

Both riches and honor come from You, and You reign over all. In Your hand is power and might; in Your hand it is to make great and to give strength to all.

Imagine the heavenly hosts worshiping Him all together! How spectacular it must be!

Nehemiah 9:5b-6

I will stand up and bless the Lord my God forever and ever! Your name is glorious! It will be exalted above all blessings and praises!

You alone are my Lord; You made heaven, the heaven of heavens, with all their hosts, the earth and everything on it, the seas and all that is in them, and You preserve them all.

The host of heaven worships You (and I worship You).

_____

_____

_____

_____

_____

Nehemiah 9:5b-6

Stand up and bless the Lord your God forever and ever! Blessed be Your glorious name, which is exalted above all blessing and praise!

You alone are the Lord; You have made heaven, the heaven of heavens, with all their hosts, the earth and everything on it, the seas and all that is in them, and You preserve them all.

The host of heaven worships You.

Psalm 62:5-8

My soul waits silently for You alone, God. All my expectations are from You. You and You only are my rock and my salvation. You are my defense; I will not be moved!

You, God, are my salvation and my glory! You are the rock of my strength and my refuge is in You, God. I will trust You at all times and pour my heart out to You, because You are my refuge!

_____

_____

_____

_____

_____

Psalm 62:5-8

My soul, wait silently for God alone, for my expectation is from Him. He only is my rock and my salvation; He is my defense; I shall not be moved.

In God is my salvation and my glory; the rock of my strength, and my refuge is in God. Trust Him at all times, you people; pour out your heart before Him; God is a refuge for us.

Psalm 84:10-12

Praise You, Lord! For a day in Your courts is better than a thousand somewhere else! I would rather be a doorkeeper in Your house than dwell in the house of the evil ones.

You, God, are my sun and shield. You, Lord, will give me grace and glory! You will not withhold any good thing from me because I walk uprightly in Your eyes!

Oh, Lord of hosts, I am blessed because I trust in You!

_____

_____

_____

_____

_____

Psalm 84:10-12

For a day in Your courts is better than a thousand. I would rather be a doorkeeper in the house of my God then dwell in the tents of wickedness.

For the Lord God is a sun and shield; the Lord will give grace and glory; no good thing will He withhold from those who walk uprightly.

Oh, Lord of hosts, blessed is the man who trusts in You!

Isaiah 12:1-6

Oh Lord, I will praise You! Though You get angry with me, Your anger is turned away and You comfort me.

You, God, are my salvation. I trust in You and I am not afraid. You, Lord, are my strength and song. You are my salvation!

With joy I will draw water from the wells of my salvation! I will praise You, my Lord! I will call upon Your name! I will declare Your deeds to anyone who listens.

Your name I will exalt! I sing to You, Lord, for You have done excellent things! I will shout for joy, for You are great! O Holy One of Israel, You are always with me!

_____

_____

_____

_____

_____

Isaiah 12:1-6

A hymn of praise

And in that day you will say: oh Lord, I will praise You; though You were angry with me, Your anger is turned away, and You comfort me.

Behold, God is my salvation, I will trust and not be afraid; For Yah, the Lord, is my strength and song; He also has become my salvation. Therefore with joy you will draw water from the wells of salvation.

And in that day you will say: praise the Lord, call upon His name; declare His deeds among the people, make mention that His name is exalted. Sing to the Lord, for He has done excellent things; this is known in all the earth.

Cry out and shout, O inhabitant of Zion, for great is the Holy One of Israel in your midst!

Isaiah 42:5b-6

God my Lord, You created the heavens and stretched them out, You spread forth the earth and that which comes from it, You give me breath; You give me spirit.

You, Lord, have called me in righteousness! You will hold my hand and keep me. You have made me a light to those outside Your family.

_____

_____

_____

_____

_____

Isaiah 42:5b-6

Thus says God the Lord, who created the heavens and stretched them out, who spread forth the earth and that which comes from it, who gives breath to the people on it, and spirit to those who walk on it:

I, the Lord, have called you in righteousness, and will hold Your hand; I will keep You and give You as a covenant to the people, as a light to the Gentiles.

Isaiah 60:19-21

The sun will not be my light, and the moon will not shine for me; but You, Lord, are my everlasting light! You, God, are my glory! You, Lord, will be my everlasting light!

The days of mourning shall be ended! I am righteous before You. I am a branch for Your planting; I am the work of Your hands! I will give You the glory!

_____

_____

_____

_____

_____

Isaiah 60: 19-21

God the glory of his people

The sun shall no longer be your light by day, nor for brightness shall the moon give light to you; but the Lord will be to you and everlasting light, and your God your glory.

Your sun shall no longer go down, nor shall your moon withdraw itself; for the Lord will be your everlasting light, and the days of your morning shall be ended.

Also your people shall be righteous; they shall inherit the land forever, the branch of My planting, the work of My hands, that I may be glorified.

Romans 8:24-29

Dear Lord, I am so grateful for the hope that I can see (like the snow that is coming down as I write this). For in hope I am saved, but hope that I can see is not hope. Why should I hope for what I can see? If I hope for what I do not see, I eagerly wait for it with perseverance.

I pray that Your Spirit helps me in my weaknesses. I do not know what I should pray for, but Your spirit makes intercession for me with groanings which cannot be uttered, according to the will of God.

Search my heart; You know what the mind of the Spirit is, and You make intercession for me.

I know that all things work together for good (for me), because I love You. Because I am called according to Your purposes. Because You foreknew me, You also predestined me to be conformed to the image of Your Son.

(To You be the glory, forever and ever! Amen!)

_____

_____

_____

_____

_____

Romans 8:24-29

For we were saved in this hope, but hope that is seen is not hope; for why does one still hope for what he sees? But if we hope for what we do not see, we eagerly wait for it with perseverance.

Likewise, the Spirit also helps in our weaknesses. For we do not know what we should pray for as we ought, but the Spirit Himself makes intercession for us with groanings which cannot be uttered.

Now He who searches the hearts knows what the mind of the Spirit is, because He makes intercession for the saints according to the will of God.

And we know that all things work together for good to those who love God, to those who are the called according to His purpose. For whom He foreknew, He also predestined to be conformed to the image of His Son, that He might be the firstborn among many brethren.

Ephesians 5:18-20

Because I am filled with the Spirit, I will write to Your holy ones with books of prayers and praises (here is the first one!), and I will keep Your Word hidden in my heart!

I give thanks to You always for all things, God my father!

_____

_____

_____

_____

_____

Ephesians 5:18-20

But be filled with the Spirit, speaking to one another in Psalms and hymns and spiritual songs, singing and making melody in your heart to the Lord,

giving thanks always for all things to God the Father in the name of our Lord Jesus Christ.

Hebrews 11:6

But without faith, it is impossible to please You, God. When I come to You, I believe that You are God, and that You reward me when I diligently seek You!

Praise to You, God!

_____

_____

_____

_____

_____

Hebrews 11:6

But without faith it is impossible to please Him, for He who comes to God must believe that He is, and that He is a rewarder of those who diligently seek Him.

Isaiah 45:22

I look to You and I am saved. Because You are (the one true) God, and there is no other!

_____

_____

_____

_____

_____

Isaiah 45:22

Look to Me, and be saved, all you ends of the earth! For I am God, and there is no other.

Deuteronomy 32:3-4

I proclaim Your name, Lord. I ascribe greatness to You, my God! You are my rock; Your works are perfect!

All Your ways are justified; You are a God of truth and without injustice. Righteous and upright You are!

_____

_____

_____

_____

_____

Deuteronomy 32:3-4

For I proclaim the name of the Lord: ascribe greatness to our God. He is the rock, His work is perfect; for all His ways are justice, a God of truth and without injustice; righteous and upright is He.

Revelation 21:3-5

(A little taste of heaven.)

You will dwell with me. I am Yours and You, God, are mine! You will personally wipe away every tear from my eyes.

I will not see death, nor sorrow, nor crying, and I will feel no more pain! For the former things have passed away! (You will make all things new!)

_____

_____

_____

_____

_____

Revelation 21:3-5

And I heard a loud voice from heaven saying, behold, the tabernacle of God is with men, and he will dwell with them, and they shall be his people.

God himself will be with them and be their God. And God will wipe away every tear from their eyes; there shall be no more death, nor sorrow, nor crying.

There shall be no more pain, for the former things have passed away.

Hymns

And Can it Be? | Be Thou My Vision
It is Well | Holy, Holy, Holy |

Just a note about these songs: I took the liberty to change some of these words to make them more personal as well.

*****

And Can it Be?

Charles Wesley (1707 – 1788)

And can it be that I should gain
an interest in my Savior's blood,
You died for me who caused Your pain.
For me, who You to death pursued!
Amazing love! How can it be?
That You, my God, should die for me?
Amazing love how can it be?
That You my God would die for me!

'Tis mystery all! The immortal dies;
who can explore Your strange design?
In vain the firstborn seraph tries
to sound the depths of love divine!
Your mercy all! Let earth adore!
Let angel minds inquire no more!
Amazing love how can it be?
That You my God would die for me!

You left Your Father's throne above
so free, so infinite Your grace,
emptied Yourself of all but love,
and bled for Adam's helpless race!
Your mercy all, immense and free!
For O my God, You found out me!
Amazing love how can it be?
That You my God would die for me!

Long my imprisoned spirit lay,
fast bound in sin and nature's night;
Your eye diffused a quickening ray,
I woke, that dungeon flamed with light!
My chains fell off! My heart was free!
I rose, went forth, and followed Thee.
Amazing love how can it be?
That You my God would die for me!

No condemnation now I dread;
You, Jesus, and all in You, are mine!
Alive in You, my living head,
and clothed in righteousness divine,
Bold I approach the eternal throne
and claim the crown through You my own!
Amazing love how can it be?
That You, My God, would die for me!?!

*****

Be Thou My Vision
Eleanor H. Hill 1912

Be Thou my vision, O Lord of my heart,
Naught be all else to me save that Thou art;
Thou my best thought by day or by night,
waking or sleeping, Thy presence my light.

Be Thou my wisdom and Thou my true word,
I ever with Thee and Thou with me, Lord;
Thou my great Father and I Thy true son,
Thou in me dwelling and I with Thee one.

Be Thou my battle shield, sword for the fight;
be Thou my dignity, Thou my delight;
Thou my soul's shelter, Thou my high tower
raise Thou me heaven ward, O power of my power.

Riches I heed not, nor man's empty praise!
Thou my inheritance now and always!
Thou and Thou only first in my heart
High King of heaven my treasure Thou art.

High King of Heaven, my victory won,
may I reach heaven's joys, oh bright heaven sun!
Heart of my own heart, whatever be fall,
still be my vision, O Ruler of all!

It is Well
Horatio G Spofford 1873

When peace like a River, attendeth my way,
when sorrows like sea billows roll:
whatever my lot, You have taught me to say,
"It is well, it is well with my soul!"

Though Satan should buffet, though trials should come,
let this blest assurance control:
That You have regarded my helpless estate
and have shed Your own blood for my soul!

My sin, oh the bliss of this glorious thought
my sin, not the part, but the whole,
is nailed to the cross, and I bear it no more!
Praise the Lord! Praise the Lord! O my soul!

And Lord, haste the day when the faith shall be sight!
The clouds be rolled back as a scroll!
The trump shall resound, and the Lord shall descend!
Even so, it is well with my soul!

It is well, with my soul;
it is well, it is well, with my soul!

Holy, Holy, Holy

Reginald Heber and John B. Dykes

Holy, holy, holy! Lord God Almighty!
Early in the morning our song shall rise to You.
Holy, holy, holy! Merciful and mighty,
God in three persons, blessed Trinity!

Holy, holy, holy! All the saints adore You,
Casting down their golden crowns around the glassy sea;
Cherubim and seraphim falling down before You,
Which were, and are, and evermore shall be?

Holy, holy, holy! Though the darkness hide You,
Though the eye of sinful man Your glory may not see,
Only You are holy; there is none beside You,
Perfect in power, in love and purity.

Holy, holy, holy! Lord God Almighty!
All Your works shall praise Your name, in earth and sky and sea.
Holy, holy, holy! Merciful and mighty,
God in three persons, blessed Trinity.

*****

The end

(for now).

Thank you for reading my first book. If you enjoyed it, won't you please take a moment to leave me a review at your favorite retailer?

It would help a lot.

Thanks!

Lorie

If you believe that this concept will help you get closer to God, then please consider joining our Daily Devotional Fellowship.

This is a group of like-minded seekers reading and reflecting on a verse or passage each day. Of course, we explore these verses from the first person perspective.

For more information, please go to

www.ScriptureInFirstPerson.com/DDF

I look forward to seeing you there.

About the Author

Lorie Forrest has been a Christian for over 20 years and has had her share of dark times and doubt, of separation and fears; but God has kept hold of her the whole time!

She says, "In these times, I was the one who turned away, not Him. He was just waiting." She lives with her husband, Dean, who reminds her that this life is not all there is.

She has 3 adult children and 10 ¾ grandchildren, and she sees them all the time! She enjoys baking and cooking.

She has a dog (who just won't stay off the couch) and currently lives in Progreso, Mexico.

Other Books by Lorie Forrest

The Gospel: ALIVE and Off the Page – This one is free!

Scripture in First Person: God's Love For Us, Coming Soon

Scripture in First Person: Prayers and Praises, Coming Soon

Please visit with me:

website www.ScriptureInFirstPerson.com

blog ScriptureInFirstPerson.com/ScriptureIsALIVE/

Index

www.ingramcontent.com/pod-product-compliance
Lightning Source LLC
Chambersburg PA
CBHW071530040426
42452CB00008B/953